SPORTS RECORDS

THE GREATEST HOCKEY RECORDS

BY MATT DOEDEN

CONSULTANT:
Roger A. Godin
Curator, Minnesota Wild
St. Paul, Minnesota

Capstone
press®

Mankato, Minnesota

Edge Books are published by Capstone Press,
151 Good Counsel Drive, P.O. Box 669, Mankato, Minnesota 56002.
www.capstonepress.com

Library of Congress Cataloging-in-Publication Data
Doeden, Matt.
    The greatest hockey records / by Matt Doeden.
    p. cm. — (Edge books. Sports records)
    Summary: "Short stories and tables of statistics describe the history and
greatest records of the National Hockey League" — Provided by publisher.
    Includes bibliographical references and index.
    ISBN-13: 978-1-4296-2008-6 (hardcover)
    ISBN-10: 1-4296-2008-0 (hardcover)
    1. Hockey — Records — Juvenile literature. 2. National Hockey
League — Juvenile Literature. I. Title. II. Series.
GV847.5.D64 2009
796.962 — dc22   2008002037

Editorial Credits

Aaron Sautter, editor; Bobbi J. Wyss, designer; Jo Miller, photo researcher

Photo Credits

AP Images, 22; Ann Heisenfelt, 28; Charles Krupa, 16; *Detroit Free Press*, 26;
    Jonathan Hayward, CP, 7
Getty Images Inc./Bruce Bennett Studios, cover (bottom right, top left), 4, 6,
    12, 14, 18, 20, 24; Melchior DiGiacomo, 10
Hockey Hall of Fame Archives, 8
Shutterstock/Graca Victoria, cover (top right); Khafizov Ivan Harisovich, cover
    (bottom left); kml, cover (middle right)

Records in this book are current through the 2007–08 regular season.

1 2 3 4 5 6 13 12 11 10 09 08

TABLE OF CONTENTS

CHAPTER 1

THE GREAT ONES

LEARN ABOUT
- Gretzky's Big Game
- NHL History
- Hockey All-Stars

4

Wayne Gretzky broke the single-season goal record with this shot in 1982.

It was February 24, 1982. The Buffalo Sabres were taking on the powerful Edmonton Oilers. But everyone's eyes were on the Oilers' young Wayne Gretzky. The 21-year-old center needed just one goal to break the single-season record.

The Sabres held Gretzky scoreless in the first two periods. But the great young player broke out in the third. Gretzky stole the puck and darted down the ice. He fired a hard shot that sailed past the goalie and into the net. With that score, Gretzky broke Phil Esposito's season record of 76 goals. Gretzky would add two more goals before the game was over. By the season's end, Gretzky had destroyed Esposito's mark with a total of 92 goals. It's a record many hockey experts believe will never be broken.

HOCKEY'S HEROES

The National Hockey League (NHL) has a long, rich history. The NHL's greats have been thrilling fans since the league started in 1917. The league started with just four teams, each playing 22-game seasons. All of the original teams were from Canada.

Gordie Howe (center) was known as "Mr. Hockey" and played for a record 32 seasons.

During the league's early years, fans cheered for Joe Malone, George Hainsworth, and other favorite players. Over the years, the game changed. Some teams moved to different cities. Schedules got longer. Rules changed. By the 1960s, a new generation of players became popular. Big-name stars like Gordie Howe and Bobby Hull set new records nobody thought could be broken.

But things soon changed again. In 1972, the World Hockey Association (WHA) formed to compete with the NHL. The two leagues competed for the fans' attention through the 1970s. By 1979, the two leagues agreed to join together to form the modern NHL. The merger brought new talent into the NHL, including a young Wayne Gretzky. The league's popularity soon exploded. In recent years, stars like Mario Lemieux and Sidney Crosby have increased fans' interest even more. These players and others continue to set great hockey records that the fans will never forget.

Sidney Crosby is one of the NHL's fastest-rising stars.

CHAPTER 2

HOCKEY'S
GREATEST PLAYERS

LEARN ABOUT

- Goals and Points
- Gutsy Defenders
- Great Goalies

Joe Malone was one of hockey's greatest stars in the NHL's early years.

When it comes to scoring, Wayne Gretzky holds almost all of the records. He holds the single-season and career records for goals, assists, and total points.

MOST GOALS IN A GAME

7	Joe Malone	1920, Quebec Bulldogs
6	Joe Malone	1920, Quebec Bulldogs
6	Newsy Lalonde	1920, Montreal Canadiens
6	Corb Denneny	1921, Toronto St. Patricks
6	Cy Denneny	1921, Ottawa Senators
6	Syd Howe	1944, Detroit Red Wings
6	Red Berenson	1968, St. Louis Blues
6	Darryl Sittler	1976, Toronto Maple Leafs

MOST GOALS IN A SEASON

92	Wayne Gretzky	1981–82, Edmonton Oilers
87	Wayne Gretzky	1983–84, Edmonton Oilers
86	Brett Hull	1990–91, St. Louis Blues
85	Mario Lemieux	1988–89, Pittsburgh Penguins
76	Phil Esposito	1970–71, Boston Bruins
76	Alexander Mogilny	1992–93, Buffalo Sabres
76	Teemu Selanne	1992–93, Winnipeg Jets

MOST CAREER GOALS

894	Wayne Gretzky	Edmonton, Los Angeles, St. Louis, N.Y. Rangers
801	Gordie Howe	Detroit, Hartford
741	Brett Hull	Calgary, St. Louis, Dallas, Detroit, Phoenix
731	Marcel Dionne	Detroit, Los Angeles, N.Y. Rangers
717	Phil Esposito	Chicago, Boston, N.Y. Rangers

"THE PHANTOM" GETS SEVEN

One scoring mark Gretzky couldn't crack was the single-game goals record. Joe Malone, nicknamed "The Phantom," set that record on January 31, 1920. Malone scored a stunning seven goals while leading the Quebec Bulldogs to a 10-6 win over the Toronto St. Patricks. It's a feat no NHL player has ever matched. And if that wasn't enough, Malone had a six-goal game later that same season.

> *Bobby Orr was known for his accurate passing and scoring ability.*

OFFENSIVE DEFENDERS

Defensemen aren't usually known for their offense, but Boston Bruin legend Bobby Orr wasn't a typical defenseman. His laser-fast shots and perfect passes made him a force at both ends of the rink. In the 1970–71 season, he collected 37 goals and 102 assists, for a total of 139 points. It's the most any defenseman has ever scored.

Edmonton's Paul Coffey took a run at Orr's record in 1985–86. However, with 48 goals and 90 assists, his point total of 138 came up just short.

MOST ASSISTS IN A SEASON

163	Wayne Gretzky	1985–86, Edmonton Oilers
135	Wayne Gretzky	1984–85, Edmonton Oilers
125	Wayne Gretzky	1982–83, Edmonton Oilers
122	Wayne Gretzky	1990–91, Los Angeles Kings
121	Wayne Gretzky	1986–87, Edmonton Oilers

MOST CAREER ASSISTS

1,963	Wayne Gretzky	Edmonton, Los Angeles, St. Louis, N.Y. Rangers
1,249	Ron Francis	Hartford, Pittsburgh, Carolina, Toronto
1,193	Mark Messier	Edmonton, N.Y. Rangers, Vancouver
1,169	Raymond Bourque	Boston, Colorado
1,135	Paul Coffey	Edmonton, Pittsburgh, Los Angeles, Detroit, Hartford, Philadelphia, Chicago, Carolina, Boston

MOST POINTS IN A SEASON

215	Wayne Gretzky	1985–86, Edmonton Oilers
212	Wayne Gretzky	1981–82, Edmonton Oilers
208	Wayne Gretzky	1984–85, Edmonton Oilers
205	Wayne Gretzky	1983–84, Edmonton Oilers
199	Mario Lemieux	1988–89, Pittsburgh Penguins

MOST CAREER POINTS

2,857	Wayne Gretzky	Edmonton, Los Angeles, St. Louis, N.Y. Rangers
1,887	Mark Messier	Edmonton, N.Y. Rangers, Vancouver
1,850	Gordie Howe	Detroit, Hartford
1,798	Ron Francis	Hartford, Pittsburgh, Carolina, Toronto
1,771	Marcel Dionne	Detroit, Los Angeles, N.Y. Rangers

EDGE FACT

In hockey, points are different between players and teams. Players get points for both goals and assists. For teams, points are what count in the standings. A team gets two points for winning a game. The losing team gets zero points. But if a game goes into overtime, the losing team still earns one point.

Patrick Roy's goaltending skills led his teams to four Stanley Cup titles.

RACKING UP THE WINS

Patrick Roy entered the NHL with a bang. In his **rookie** season, 1985–86, he led the Montreal Canadiens to a Stanley Cup title. He was named MVP of the Stanley Cup Finals at age 20. Roy was a goaltender with a great feel for the game. He seemed to know just where an opposing player was going to shoot the puck.

rookie — a first-year player

MOST CAREER GOALTENDING WINS – REGULAR SEASON

551	Patrick Roy	Montreal, Colorado
534	Martin Brodeur	New Jersey
484	Ed Belfour	Chicago, San Jose, Dallas, Toronto, Florida
447	Terry Sawchuk	Detroit, Boston, Toronto, Los Angeles, N.Y. Rangers
446	Curtis Joseph	St. Louis, Edmonton, Toronto, Detroit, Phoenix, Calgary

MOST CAREER GOALTENDING WINS – PLAYOFFS

151	Patrick Roy	Montreal, Colorado
94	Martin Brodeur	New Jersey
92	Grant Fuhr	Edmonton, Toronto, Buffalo, Los Angeles, St. Louis, Calgary
88	Billy Smith	Los Angeles, N.Y. Islanders
88	Ed Belfour	Chicago, San Jose, Dallas, Toronto, Florida

MOST GOALTENDING SHUTOUTS IN A SEASON

22	George Hainsworth	1928–29, Montreal Canadiens
15	Alex Connell	1925–26, Ottawa Senators
15	Alex Connell	1927–28, Ottawa Senators
15	Hal Winkler	1927–28, Boston Bruins
15	Tony Esposito	1969–70, Chicago Blackhawks

MOST CAREER GOALTENDING SHUTOUTS

103	Terry Sawchuck	Detroit, Boston, Toronto, Los Angeles, N. Y. Rangers
96	Martin Brodeur	New Jersey
94	George Hainsworth	Montreal, Toronto
84	Glenn Hall	Detroit, Chicago, St. Louis
82	Jacques Plante	Montreal, N.Y. Rangers, St. Louis, Toronto, Boston

Roy's skills earned him a lot of wins. On October 17, 2000, he got the 448th win of his career, passing the record held by Terry Sawchuk. Roy retired in 2003 with a record 551 career victories. He also holds the record for playoff wins with 151.

Doug Jarvis didn't miss a single game in 12 straight seasons.

HOCKEY'S "IRON MAN"

Hockey is a tough, bruising sport. Broken bones, twisted ankles, and knocked-out teeth are all part of the game. But for center Doug Jarvis, missing a game was never an option. Jarvis played from 1975 to 1987. In that time, he didn't miss a single game. At 964 **consecutive** games, Jarvis is the NHL's all-time "Iron Man."

14

consecutive — when something happens several times in a row without a break

MOST CONSECUTIVE GAMES PLAYED

964	Doug Jarvis	1975–1987
914	Garry Unger	1968–1979
884	Steve Larmer	1982–1993
776	Craig Ramsay	1973–1982
630	Andy Hebenton	1955–1964

MOST CAREER GAMES PLAYED

1,767	Gordie Howe	Detroit, Hartford
1,756	Mark Messier	Edmonton, N.Y. Rangers, Vancouver
1,731	Ron Francis	Hartford, Pittsburgh, Carolina, Toronto
1,639	Dave Andreychuk	Buffalo, Toronto, New Jersey, Boston, Colorado, Tampa Bay
1,635	Scott Stevens	Washington, St. Louis, New Jersey

Goaltender Glen Hall was another iron man. From 1954 to 1963, he tended goal in 502 straight games. And every one of them was a complete game. He never took a rest until a back injury forced him out in game number 503.

15

EDGE FACT

Toronto's Darryl Sittler holds the record for points scored in a single game. He scored a total of 10 points on February 7, 1976. Sittler scored six goals and had four assists in an 11-4 win over Boston.

CHAPTER 3

HOCKEY'S
GREATEST TEAMS

LEARN ABOUT

- Dominant Teams
- Winning Streaks
- Stanley Cup Titles

The Detroit Red Wings (right) were almost unbeatable during the 1995–96 season.

16

Watching great players set records is exciting. But hockey is a team game. Over the years, hockey teams have achieved many notable records.

MOST WINS IN A SEASON

62	Detroit Red Wings	1995–96
60	Montreal Canadiens	1976–77
59	Montreal Canadiens	1977–78

MOST POINTS IN A SEASON

132	Montreal Canadiens	1976–77
131	Detroit Red Wings	1995–96
129	Montreal Canadiens	1977–78

BEST POINTS PERCENTAGE IN A SEASON

.875	Boston Bruins	1929–30
.830	Montreal Canadiens	1943–44
.825	Montreal Canadiens	1976–77
.806	Montreal Canadiens	1977–78
.800	Montreal Canadiens	1944–45

A SEASON TO REMEMBER

Which team had the greatest season in NHL history? The 1995–96 Detroit Red Wings hold the record for the most wins with 62. But in the 1976–77 season, the Montreal Canadiens had more tie games. The Canadiens ended their season with a total of 132 points, one more than Detroit.

However, neither Detroit nor Montreal hold the record for the best points percentage. That's the percentage of possible points that a team can earn in a season. The 1929–30 Boston Bruins hold the single-season percentage record. The Bruins went 38-5-1 that season. They earned 77 out of a possible 88 points that season, giving them a points percentage of .875.

17

STREAKING TO SUCCESS

In 1993, Mario Lemieux and Jaromir Jagr led an almost unbeatable Pittsburgh Penguins team. The Penguins won a record 17 games in a row from March 9 to April 10.

18

EDGE FACT

In 1980, the Winnipeg Jets went 30 games without a win. From October 19 to December 20, they lost 23 games and tied 7. It's the longest winless streak in NHL history.

LONGEST WINNING STREAKS, REGULAR SEASON

17	Pittsburgh Penguins	1993
15	New York Islanders	1982
14	Boston Bruins	1929–30

LONGEST WINNING STREAKS, PLAYOFFS

14	Pittsburgh Penguins	1993
12	Edmonton Oilers	1985

OTHER WINNING STREAKS

Longest unbeaten streak:	35	Philadelphia Flyers	1979–80
Longest unbeaten streak to start season:	15	Edmonton Oilers	1984
Longest winning streak to start season:	10	Toronto Maple Leafs	1993
Longest home winning streak:	20	Boston Bruins and	1929–30
		Philadelphia Flyers	1976
Longest road winning streak:	12	Detroit Red Wings	2006

But the Philadelphia Flyers had an even greater **streak**. From October 14, 1979, to January 6, 1980, the team didn't lose a single game. With 25 wins and 10 ties, their 35-game unbeaten streak is the longest in history. And since the NHL no longer has tie games, it's one record that will probably never be broken.

19

streak — an unbroken series of games

A SCORING MACHINE

The Edmonton Oilers were a scoring machine during the mid-1980s. With stars like Wayne Gretzky, Mark Messier, and Paul Coffey, the Oilers scored goals like no team in NHL history. In 1983–84, they tallied 446 goals, beating their own record of 424 set the season before.

AVERAGE GOALS-PER-GAME SCORED IN A SEASON

5.58	Edmonton Oilers	1983–84
5.38	Montreal Canadiens	1919–20
5.33	Edmonton Oilers	1985–86
5.23	Edmonton Oilers	1982–83

AVERAGE GOALS-PER-GAME ALLOWED IN A SEASON

0.98	Montreal Canadiens	1928–29
1.09	Montreal Canadiens	1927–28
1.17	Ottawa Senators	1925–26
1.18	Boston Bruins	1928–29

OTHER TEAM RECORDS

Most goals in a season:	446	Edmonton Oilers	1983–84
Most goals in a game:	16	Montreal Canadiens	1920
Most shots in a game:	83	Boston Bruins	1941
Most penalties in a game:	44	Edmonton Oilers	1990
Most penalty minutes in a season:	2,713	Buffalo Sabres	1991–92

Defense is just as important as offense. The 1925–26 Ottawa Senators were one of the best defensive teams ever. They only allowed 42 goals to be scored on them that season. The 1928–29 Montreal Canadiens were even better, though. They allowed one more goal than the Senators, but they played eight more games that season.

21

EDGE FACT

The record for the most scoring in a regular season game is 21 goals. It's happened twice. In 1920, Montreal beat Toronto 14-7. Then Edmonton topped Chicago 12-9 in 1985.

WINNING IT ALL

The goal of every NHL team is to play in the Stanley Cup Finals. From 1951 to 1960, the Montreal Canadiens reached that goal a record 10 straight years. Forward Maurice Richard led the team to six titles during that span. These included a record five in a row from 1956 to 1960. That amazing stretch made the Canadiens the most successful team in Stanley Cup history. With a record of 23 NHL titles, no other team even comes close.

The Montreal Canadiens were almost unbeatable during the late 1950s.

MOST STANLEY CUP TITLES

23	Montreal Canadiens	1924, 1930–31, 1944, 1946, 1953, 1956–60, 1965–66, 1968–69, 1971, 1973, 1976–79, 1986, 1993
13	Toronto Maple Leafs	1918, 1922, 1932, 1942, 1945, 1947–49, 1951, 1962–64, 1967
10	Detroit Red Wings	1936–37, 1943, 1950, 1952, 1954–55, 1997–98, 2002
5	Boston Bruins	1929, 1939, 1941, 1970, 1972
5	Edmonton Oilers	1984–85, 1987–88, 1990

MOST CONSECUTIVE STANLEY CUP TITLES

5	Montreal Canadiens	1956–1960
4	Montreal Canadiens	1976–1979
4	New York Islanders	1980–1983

PLAYOFF RECORDS

Most goals in a playoff series:	44	Edmonton Oilers	1985
Most goals in a playoff game:	13	Edmonton Oilers	1987
Most goals in a playoff period:	7	Montreal Canadiens	1944
Most penalties in a playoff game:	34	Minnesota North Stars	1990

EDGE FACT

The Boston Bruins hold the record for the most consecutive playoff appearances. They made the playoffs every season from 1968 to 1996. That's 29 straight years!

CHAPTER 4

HOCKEY'S WILDEST RECORDS

LEARN ABOUT
- A Rare Achievement
- A Really Long Game
- Fast Scoring

In 1981, Wayne Gretzky scored his first 50 goals in fewer games than any NHL player in history.

50 IN 39

24

One of Wayne Gretzky's most memorable records came on December 30, 1981. He was chasing a record shared at the time by Maurice Richard and Mike Bossy. They had both scored 50 goals in the first 50 games of a season. Entering the 39th game of the season, Gretzky already had 45 goals.

MOST CONSECUTIVE GAMES WITH A GOAL

16	Punch Broadbent	1921–22, Ottawa Senators
14	Joe Malone	1917–18, Montreal Canadiens
13	Newsy Lalonde	1920–21, Montreal Canadiens
13	Charlie Simmer	1979–80, Los Angeles Kings

MOST CONSECUTIVE GAMES WITH AN ASSIST

23	Wayne Gretzky	1990–91, Los Angeles Kings
18	Adam Oates	1992–93, Boston Bruins
17	Wayne Gretzky	1983–84, Edmonton Oilers
17	Paul Coffey	1985–86, Edmonton Oilers
17	Wayne Gretzky	1989–90, Los Angeles Kings

MOST CONSECUTIVE GAMES WITH A POINT

51	Wayne Gretzky	1983–84, Edmonton Oilers
46	Mario Lemieux	1989–90, Pittsburgh Penguins
39	Wayne Gretzky	1985–86, Edmonton Oilers
30	Wayne Gretzky	1982–83, Edmonton Oilers
30	Mats Sundin	1992–93, Quebec Nordiques

That night, Gretzky exploded against the Philadelphia Flyers. He scored two goals in the first period. In the second period, he notched a **hat trick** by scoring his third goal of the game. Early in the third period, he scored his fourth goal, giving him 49. With just three seconds left in the game, Gretzky got the puck one more time. He fired it into an empty net for his fifth goal of the night. He had scored 50 goals in just 39 games. It's a record that will be very difficult to break.

hat trick — when a player scores three goals in one game

The Detroit Red Wings won both the NHL's longest game and the 1936 Stanley Cup.

A LONG, LONG GAME

In the playoffs, there are no ties or **shoot-outs**. Teams keep skating until a tie is broken. And on March 24, 1936, that meant an amazing six overtimes!

After 60 minutes of regulation hockey, Detroit and Montreal were tied at zero. The deadlock continued for one overtime after another. Finally, after more than 116 minutes of overtime, Detroit scored the game winner. The game lasted for a record-breaking seven hours on the ice. Detroit went on to win the Stanley Cup that season.

26

shoot-out — a method of breaking a tie score at the end of overtime play

LONGEST OVERTIMES IN NHL HISTORY

116:30	Detroit Red Wings 1, Montreal Maroons 0	March 24, 1936
104:46	Toronto Maple Leafs 1, Boston Bruins 0	April 3, 1933
92:01	Philadelphia Flyers 2, Pittsburgh Penguins 1	May 4, 2000
80:48	Anaheim Mighty Ducks 4, Dallas Stars 3	April 24, 2003
79:15	Pittsburgh Penguins 3, Washington Capitals 2	April 24, 1996

MOST GOALTENDING LOSSES IN A SEASON

48	Gary Smith	1970–71, California Golden Seals
47	Al Rollins	1953–54, Chicago Blackhawks
46	Peter Sidorkiewicz	1992–93, Ottawa Senators
44	Harry Lumley	1951–52, Chicago Blackhawks

MOST CAREER ALL-STAR GAMES

23	Gordie Howe	Detroit, Hartford
19	Raymond Bourque	Boston, Colorado
18	Wayne Gretzky	Edmonton, Los Angeles, St. Louis, N.Y. Rangers
15	Frank Mahovlich	Toronto, Detroit, Montreal
15	Mark Messier	Edmonton, N.Y. Rangers, Vancouver

MOST GOALS BY A ROOKIE

76	Teemu Selanne	1992–93, Winnipeg Jets
53	Mike Bossy	1977–78, New York Islanders
52	Alex Ovechkin	2005–06, Washington Capitals
51	Joe Nieuwendyk	1987–88, Calgary Flames
43	Dale Hawerchuk	1981–82, Winnipeg Jets
43	Luc Robitaille	1986–87, Los Angeles Kings

EDGE FACT

In 2006–07, 19-year-old Sidney Crosby of the Pittsburgh Penguins led the NHL with 120 points. He became the first teenager in any of the major pro sports leagues to win a scoring title.

TWO FAST SHOTS

28

On January 21, 2004, the Minnesota Wild set a record that will be tough to beat. In the closing seconds of regulation time, the Wild and the Chicago Blackhawks were tied 2-2. With 16 seconds to play, center Jim Dowd slapped a rebound into the Chicago net.

FASTEST GOALS

Fastest goal scored from the start of a game: 5 SECONDS

Doug Smail	1981, Winnipeg Jets
Bryan Trottier	1984, New York Islanders
Alexander Mogilny	1991, Buffalo Sabres

Fastest goal scored by a player in his first NHL game: 15 SECONDS

Gus Bodnar	1943, Toronto Maple Leafs

Fastest two goals scored from start of game by one player: 27 SECONDS

Mike Knuble	2003, Boston Bruins

FIRSTS AND LASTS

Player to score 150 or more points in a season:

First:	Phil Esposito	**152 POINTS**	1970–71, Boston Bruins
Last:	Mario Lemieux	**161 POINTS**	1995–96, Pittsburgh Penguins

Player to score 75 or more goals in a season:

First:	Phil Esposito	**76 GOALS**	1970–71, Boston Bruins
Last:	Alexander Mogilny	**76 GOALS**	1992–93, Buffalo Sabres
	and Teemu Selanne	**76 GOALS**	1992–93, Winnipeg Jets

The Blackhawks then pulled their goalie for an extra skater. But the Wild won the face-off. The puck went to winger Richard Park. He fired a quick, hard shot that went into the empty net. The goal came just three seconds after Dowd's goal. The Wild had just scored the fastest two goals by one team in NHL history.

Hockey is a game of speed, power, and skill. Fans love watching powerful slapshots, amazing saves, and bone-crunching checks. They never know when hockey's greatest records might be broken to make new NHL history.

GLOSSARY

assist (uh-SIST) — a pass that leads to a score by a teammate

center (SEN-tur) — the player who participates in a face-off at the beginning of play

consecutive (kuhn-SEK-yuh-tiv) — when something happens several times in a row without a break

face-off (FAYSS-awf) — when a player from each team battles for possession of the puck to start or restart play

forward (FOR-wurd) — a player whose main job is to move the puck toward the opponent's goal and try to score goals

hat trick (HAT TRIK) — when a player scores three goals in one game

points percentage (POINTZ pur-SEN-tij) — the percentage of total possible points a team can earn in a season

rookie (RUK-ee) — a first-year player

shoot-out (SHOOT-out) — a method of breaking a tie score at the end of overtime play

streak (STREEK) — an unbroken series of games

READ MORE

DeCock, Luke. *Great Teams in Hockey History*. Great Teams. Chicago: Raintree, 2006.

Doeden, Matt. *Wayne Gretzky*. Sports Heroes and Legends. Minneapolis: Twenty-First Century Books, 2008.

Kennedy, Mike. *Ice Hockey*. Watts Library. New York: Franklin Watts, 2003.

INTERNET SITES

FactHound offers a safe, fun way to find Internet sites related to this book. All of the sites on FactHound have been researched by our staff.

Here's how:
1. Visit *www.facthound.com*
2. Choose your grade level.
3. Type in this book ID **1429620080** for age-appropriate sites. You may also browse subjects by clicking on letters, or by clicking on pictures and words.
4. Click on the **Fetch It** button.

FactHound will fetch the best sites for you!

INDEX

MAY 12 2009

Doeden, Matt
The Greatest Hockey
Records

	DATE DUE		
MAY 2 9 2009			
JUL 1 4 2009			
JUL 2 9 2009			
AUG 2 4 2009			
AUG 0 7 2012			
SEP 0 9 2013			
DEC 0 2 2014			